letters to the person i was

letters to the person i was

sana abuleil

Andrews McMeel
PUBLISHING®

letters to the person i was

Andrews McMeel Publishing
a division of Andrews McMeel Universal
1130 Walnut Street, Kansas City, Missouri 64106

www.andrewsmcmeel.com

19 20 21 22 23 SDB 10 9 8 7 6 5 4 3 2 1

ISBN: 978-1-5248-5404-1

Library of Congress Control Number: 2019947576

Editor: Katie Gould
Art Director: Tiffany Meairs
Production Editor: Jasmine Lim
Production Manager: Carol Coe
Illustrator: Brandon Pedro

for me. for every version of me.

a note from the author

let me explain.

this book is the way i say, "you didn't break me."
it's the way i look fear in the eye and tell it, "i did
what you said i couldn't. i did it, and i did it loud."

let me explain. when i was a little girl, i realized
quickly that having a heart bigger than most
meant i could carry pain heavier than most. when
i was a little girl, i was introduced to depression,
anxiety, and trauma. my best friend had begun
self-harming, and my growing mind couldn't quite
grasp the dangers of the situation. instead,
i thought i could heal her. i thought i could make
her better. i thought if i could just be there for
her, that if i could just stay on standby—day
and night—then she would be okay. so we started
a tally. one tick in my yellow notebook for every
day she could go without making herself bleed.

she never got past 87. and my heart shattered
every time. i blamed myself every time.

let me explain. i was caught in a situation where
i was setting myself up for heartbreak. where
with every fresh wound, i'd tell myself, "you
could've stopped it." but i couldn't have. i couldn't
have, and i know that now. my heart is big. but
i couldn't have.

after years of dealing with these feelings, after
years of blame and guilt and misery, i finally

began to realize that i was not responsible. that i tried my best, that i loved her wholeheartedly, and that i needed to walk away regardless. that i needed to put myself first—something i was never really taught. but something i needed to learn. and that's what this book is. it's a learning process. it's trying to work through emotions that have piled up over the course of twelve years. it is, for the first time, replaying it all in my head. willingly. it is learning what it means to forgive, what it means to move on, and what it means to love.

this book is learning that healing is not linear. that it is a back and forth pull. it is learning to be okay with it all, but also learning that not okay is okay, too. this book is where i put it all behind me.

this book is where i let it all go.

with love,

sana abuleil

may you find words here
that extinguish the fire of your pain
and keep the flame of your hope burning.

contents

i was 12.
i was not okay.
i was 12
when she picked up her first knife
dragged the blades across her skin
and watched the blood
stain the sink
with a smile on her face
and tears on mine.
i was 12
when i grew up way too fast.
i was
her punching bag
her stand-in therapist
her medication.
i was 12
when i carried the weight of the world
on my shoulders
for her.
i was 12
when my friends stopped recognizing me.
i was 12
when i stopped recognizing myself.
now
do you know what it feels like
to carry all the world's blame
in the creases of your heart?
because i do.
i was 12
when i started filling up notebooks
with the catastrophe i was.
i grew up when
i was 12.
i knew reality better than i should have.
i knew sadness better than most.

i was 12
when heartbreak stopped being a word
and started becoming a state of self.
a state of mind.
but this story
it isn't heartbreak.
it isn't helplessness
hopelessness
or misery.
this story isn't about her.
or you.
it's about me.
this story is my mind
and the tornado it is.
it is the thoughts i have pushed back
and locked away
in an empty corner of my brain
thinking they'd eventually decompose.
but i was wrong.
they only grew bigger
and stronger
until the doors couldn't handle all the weight.
this story is the words i should have said.
not to her.
or you.
but to me.

this story is healing.

the innocence

here you are. this is where you've been for
a while. this is where you're supposed to be
for now. come in. get comfortable.
we don't have much time.

03/14/2008

you're a fool for hope
a sucker for second chances.
you trust
and you believe
until you're high off a belonging
that isn't really yours to feel.
until you're drunk off cheap acceptance
that isn't actually real.
until you throw up words
that are meant for only you to hear.
but you can't help yourself
because they promise you things
you've spent too long searching for
but they lie.
and i'm sorry that you'll have to
pick up the pieces of your glass heart
on your own.

there's so much purity
in you
the way you hold out your hands
asking for more
happiness
or any happiness at all.
the way you pour rubbing alcohol
in your wounds
thinking they'll heal
that you won't have to feel them again
or see them again.
there's so much innocence
in who you are
thinking your voice is heard
thinking your words matter
thinking they might just listen
to what you have to say.
except they'll never hear you
with a voice so fragile.
but i know you'll destroy
your vocal chords
trying anyway.

04/02/2008

"i'll give you the world"
you say to all the people
you meet and learn to love.
but you keep giving
until there isn't anything
left for you.
until you feel an emptiness
inside you
that you never felt before.
until you get to know
the places in your heart
where an entire galaxy
once lived.
and you stay up
night after night
trying to fill the space
with things that cannot stay
like poetry
old love letters
and saved messages.
but the memory
of the worlds you gave away
will always remain.

05/12/2008

i don't know why
you gravitate
toward the ones
who don't know your worth.
but you do.
every time.
and maybe it's because
you don't know either
but let me tell you.
you aren't gold
and you aren't diamonds.
you're a van gogh original
your mother's old photo album.
but you keep falling in love
with people who think you're replaceable
who mistake your kindness for obligation.
who misinterpret your mind
for anything less than complex
messy
but so damn perfect.
i hope you let go of these people.
i hope you don't wait until they let go of you.

05/27/2008

you have this bad habit
of wanting
of holding your hands out
wide-eyed
expecting everyone you meet
to give you a little bit of
gentleness
warmth
and comfort.
and they do
sometimes
but it never lasts
because you have this bad habit
of wanting
more and more
never really happy
with what you get
and you don't know why.
but i do.
i think you search for things
in other people
that you'll only find in you.
and i think
it's messing with your head.

06/24/2008

the day you learn
you're on your own
will be a hard one.
when they grow tired
of your crazy
you'll wonder
why you aren't like them.
why your head isn't quiet.
why your laugh isn't louder.
but it's okay.
it's okay.
i think it'll be okay.
because i think they'll wonder
why they're not
a little more like you.

07/07/2008

i started writing this
thinking i could convince you
to sleep when the clock hits 12
because i know you're up
fingers curling
searching for a hand to hold
that's never there.
but i'm here now too
and it's 5 past 12:00
and i won't sleep either
so instead
i want to tell you that i'm proud of you
for putting yourself before them
for letting yourself hurt
if it means they'll heal
and i know it's not always a good thing
and i know it's not always a bad thing either
but there's something about your heart
the way it smiles
even when your lips can't.
so rest your head
and if you won't sleep
then we'll stay up together
and i won't let your fingers curl
around this emptiness.
i'll hold your hand until the sun rises
and you won't feel it
i know
because you haven't read my letters yet
but it's okay.
i'm here anyway.
rest your head.

you've been told
you love like whales drink ocean water
that you open too wide
take in too much
too quickly.
you've been told
that you chew off
more than you can swallow
that you love too hard
too overwhelmingly
that you spit up kindness
and no one knows what to do with it all
how to take it
remold it
and give it back
but i know you
and i know you don't want it back.
i know you don't love so you can take
you love so you can learn new ways to give.

i bet he has brown eyes
and a smile that reminds you
of the diamond ring
your father bought you
and the way his face lights up
every time you wear it.
and he probably has pretty words
and you'll most likely fall for them
because well
you have pretty words too
and you'll think it's meant to be.
he probably thinks he understands you
but i don't think he will.
i think he'll say he does
because he thinks you're easy to fool
because that's kind of
what your poetry says about you
doesn't it?
anyone who writes about worry
and heartbreak
and sadness
has to be easy to fool
otherwise there wouldn't be
much of those things
in the first place
right?
i bet you won't believe me though
because i'm still waiting to see if i'm right
to see if he really does have brown eyes
and if he does
i think i'm going to get lost in them
along with his pretty words
and the way he memorizes my poems

and i'm probably going to be devastated
when i realize it isn't really love
but i'm kind of hoping that
the one with brown eyes
will prove us both wrong
so i guess we'll figure this one out
together.

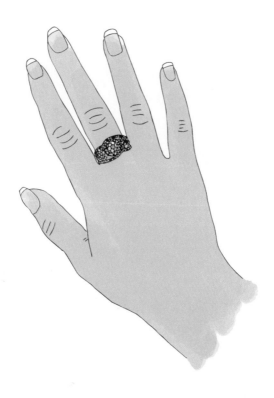

"people aren't hospitals"
you whisper to yourself
as you use
their fingers as splinters
their arms as bandages
and
their words as prescriptions.
"people can't heal you"
you keep telling yourself
as you run your fingers
through their hair
collecting strands
to turn into thread
trying to stitch cuts
that haven't healed
over the years.
"people aren't home"
you say out loud
as you're on your knees
cutting keys and installing locks
in those
that have no intention of staying
and this
this is where you keep losing yourself
and this
this is why you keep hurting.

in this part of the story
i'm supposed to tell you
about all the times
you've mistaken people
for good
when they were nowhere near
and how your naivety is beautiful
and it is
don't get me wrong
but my pages are always blank
when i try to write you this part
because i don't really remember
what it feels like
to have faith in a world
that looks like this one
and to have a piggy bank heart
taking when they give
because you think they do it out of kindness
until they break you to pieces
to take it all back.
i don't remember what it's like
but that doesn't mean i don't see good here.
i do
i do
i swear i do
even if it takes me a little longer
to find it.

the refusing

things don't change and people are good and
people are bad and people stay the same and
you are where you're supposed to be. right?

01/11/2009

and there's this pain somewhere
in your heart maybe
that will be the end of you
whether you believe me or not
because i know you can't breathe
with an entire universe
sitting on your chest
and you can't breathe
when you're in love
with an ocean
that fills your lungs with salt water
every time you inhale
but it's gotten to the point
where you'd rather drown
in love
than suffocate without it.
but there is no in between here
there never has been.
but oh
how you'll wish there was.

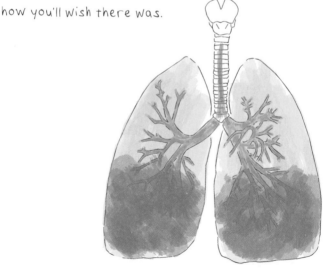

02/23/2009

she hurt you and you loved her.
but there were days
you wanted her to fall
because you thought it would change her
thought it would make her realize
that you could heal her
if only she let you
but she never did
and you wanted to play doctor anyway.
you wanted an awakening
but for who?
you wanted an awakening
but i don't know which one of you
needed it most.

05/12/2009

sometimes i think
i'm running out of things to tell you
but this book isn't finished yet
and i know that because
something in me still aches
and i don't know if it's you
screaming
"why didn't you warn me"
over and over
until my heart tries to wrap arteries
around itself
until it can't beat anymore
so i feel you
somewhere
and when i do
my tongue swells up with words
and i sit down
ready to write you these letters
but sometimes
they get caught in all my worry
because i don't know
what hearing these words will do to you.
i just hope they find you
safely
peacefully
and at a time
when you're searching for them
in everyone but yourself.

05/22/2009

i don't know what love is
but i keep talking
like i do.
writing poems
and metaphors
like love's been ingrained in me.
but it hasn't
and i really have no clue.
funny
isn't it?
i'm here and still unsure
and you're there
acting like you know
but you don't.
we don't.
at least not yet.

06/02/2009

your life's starting to look like
a black and white rubik's cube.
like no matter the algorithm
no matter how sure you are
that you've made the right moves
and calculated every consequence
you still won't know
how far you've come.
you still won't know
if you've made any progress
or if you've taken any steps back.
so now you're left
trying to figure out how to
solve a puzzle
when all the pieces blur into one another.

09/18/2009

when it's so loud
that you can't even hear
anything
because every thought
comes with so much noise
that your ears can't handle
can't process
can't even begin to understand
and you don't want them to anyway
because
no good can come from understanding
because
these thoughts
they're no good
in the first place
but it's loud
it's loud
and nothing makes it quiet
but her
and him
but they're loud
too
and you don't know what to do.

and with a mind
that looks a little bit like
a forest fire
that leaves a little more damage
than a tsunami
that ruins a few more lives
than an earthquake
he'll still look at you
and see
the abandoned building
you used to drive to
in the middle of the night
just so you could see the stars
a little more clearly.
he'll look at you
and somehow
see an entire orchestra
loud
but so damn quiet.
and he'll smile
almost as if to say
"after every rainstorm
will always come relief."
and you'll look back at him
and think
"but you are my relief.
so what does that make me?"

12/12/2009

write
read
delete
words are safe
or at least they used to be
now they're wood
strong enough to build
soft enough to burn
kind of like you
but a little more soft
and a little less strong
kind of like the home
you keep tearing down
because it never feels right
never feels like it should
never feel like you should.
write
read
delete
let your eyes talk this time
at least they can't start wildfires
at least a home only you can see
can't come apart
write
read
delete
delete
delete
always delete.

02/19/2010

you walk into an empty room
and the walls whisper and stare
because they think your loneliness is contagious.
it probably is.
cut.
next.
you walk into your childhood home
and the floor shakes in fear
because it thinks you're back for blood.
you are.
cut.
next.
you open your old journals
and the words hide behind your doodles
because they think you've finally grown a backbone.
you haven't.
cut.
next.
you're getting older
and the years are stalling
because they know you're afraid
of the future.
someone cut.
someone call next.

they'll turn you into sacred
like the empty cathedrals you'll visit
when you turn 17
on the road trip you take to nowhere.
like the locket you wear around your neck
that they call holy.
but they only want to watch you burn.
they'll turn your divine
into a garden of flames
listen to you choke on the smoke
as it fills your lungs.
they'll call you sacrificial
they'll ask you to thank them
for your burns
to thank them
because they'll say you needed
to feel the fire
because the world is an inferno.
they'll say they prepared you
for what's yet to come.
and they might have
but don't thank them for it.

03/30/2010

this is the letter you'll write
but never send.
my advice?
send it.
"mom
i'm tired
of wanting things in life
that can never be mine
of leaving chaos behind me
because i can't
ever seem to stay
long enough
to clean it all up.
mom
i wish
i'd listened to you
i wish
i hadn't seen this much
of the world
i wish
i'd let you protect me
because you tried
my god did you try.
what do i do?
how do i get over this?
mom
why didn't you make me listen?
i know you said these words
but why the hell didn't i listen?"

05/25/2010

remember the feeling of
"i've got too much happiness and
my pockets are too small
to hold it all"?
the days where you came home to
your superhero mom in the kitchen
stepping over sprawled legos
from the night before.
remember the feeling of
"i've got too much love and
my small hands can't carry it all"?
the days where you sat on your father's lap
when he came home from work
just to get a better look
at his smile
because it's always brighter up close.
but i bet you won't remember
how
in some way
somewhere
over the years
these feelings got mixed up with
"i have bags and bags of emptiness and
i can't find what i'm looking for."

06/12/2010

your heart keeps landing
in the hands of people
who have a bad habit of
taking it
whether you offer or not
chewing it up
until it's something
you no longer recognize
spitting it out
and telling you
it just wasn't quite what they were
looking for.

you've been trying to find
a dictionary definition
for the word
toxic
because it seems to be stamped
all over your life
and everyone in it
and i thought you knew what it meant
i thought you memorized it
studied its meaning
and wrote journals and reviews
on the way it's come to life
and you did
you did
but you haven't learned a thing
because you still seem to be a magnet
for everything toxic
and i'm starting to think
it's because
you've been studying this word
like it's a window
when it's been a mirror
all along.

and it's funny because
i don't know
if i want to write this one anymore
not the poem
or the chapter
but the whole damn book
and every time i feel this way
i tell myself
"this is what you've become
someone who can never finish anything
who jumps so deep into everything
only to realize you can't even swim
so to save yourself
you drown everyone who jumped with you
and this is why love
and everything else
always feels like dying."

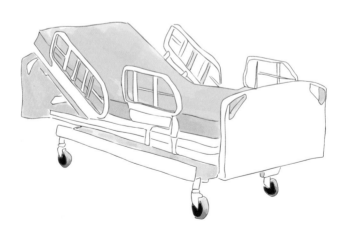

you can't find a way
to make love sit comfortably
in your mouth
kind of like when
you've been chewing gum for too long
and your tongue
doesn't know where to put it anymore.
you've been chewing love for too long
and it tastes a little different
every day
but never quite right.
you can never seem to figure out
what to do with it
when you have it
and when you don't
it's the only thing you crave.

love runs out.
but in ways you wouldn't expect.
kind of like when you finally get to bed
after a day of giving
too much time
too much energy
too much you
and your body falls into itself
trying to recall where it all went
how you spent it
and why you weren't more responsible.
love runs out.
i wish i could tell you it didn't
but you can only give so much
before you're walking around town
with too many i-owe-yous to count.
trust me.
i'm still paying off my debts.

you always wonder why everyone
speaks louder than you
why they're more full of calendars
and hope.
and you wonder
whether or not they know about
how the world will ruin them
how some mountains can never be moved
and how some people can never be changed.
and you worry because
you know someone needs to break it to them
but you don't want to see their faces
when they hear about the venom
that sometimes lives where happiness should
and you worry because
you don't want to hear their quietness
when they learn about all the people
who pretend to have warm hearts
just to lure you in
and watch you play with fire.
you don't want to be the one
to break it to them
and i never wanted to be the one
to break it to you either.
but if i didn't
who would?
and if you don't
who will?

you collect words
like someone's got your tongue
as if you don't have any of your own
and can't speak for yourself.
but you can and you know it.
you keep collecting words
like poetry isn't your first language
as if you don't think in metaphors
and can't use your pen
to make them feel.
but you can and you know it.
you collect words
but i wish you would stop
because if your emptiness
is filled with these things
then where are you going to go
with the pieces of yourself that you leave
in everything you write?
what are you going to do
when you flip through old journals
to take back what they stole?

what if i told you that life isn't
two roads diverged in a yellow wood
that instead it's one big casino
where you either lose
everything you have
or everything you are
like a poker game
with a rigged deck of cards
and a face that tells more
than your mouth ever could.
what if i told you that
you could speak
until your words
slur into one another
until your lungs
beg you for a break
and they still won't hear you
won't listen
to a thing you have to say
but somehow
still criticize your silence.
what if i told you that life isn't
two roads diverged in a yellow wood
that there is no path less travelled
and that instead
life's a cheat
a player with cards up its sleeves
and you are new to this
and you don't stand a chance.

06/17/2011

i think i'm dying again
but you don't have to worry
i still need to write you these letters
so you don't think it's the end
when you wake up to a tug-of-war match
between your lungs and the air around you.
you don't have to worry
because it isn't really dying
if they say it's in your head right?
like if you kill a character
in those stories
you never let anyone read
is it really murder?
is this really dying?
or is this more like the sound a tree makes
when it falls in an empty forest
but does this still count as a riddle
if you're the one who cut the tree down
or if your screams drown out the sound?
i think i'm dying again
but you don't have to worry.
the forest is nowhere near empty
every version of who i am
since you
is here
there are hundreds of me
but i still can't tell you my last name
or where i came from
or where i'm going.
i think i'm dying again.

after caitlyn siehl's "noah"

sometimes you catch glimpses of broken
kind of like the way the light
shines through closed blinds
forceful and persistent.
you're forceful and persistent
or at least you're trying to be
but this broken
keeps getting in the way.
sometimes you feel a type of tiredness
that makes its way into your mind.
i imagine it comes in a glass-bottom boat
through your veins
taking breaks every now and then
getting lost in parts of you
that aren't really part of you
and you don't know
who they belong to
or how they've sewn themselves
to your insides
but you feel them
and sometimes they're loud
and overpowering
until it starts to look a lot like
a tug-of-war match
between what you are
and what they want you to be
and what you want to be
is stuck on the sidelines
too afraid to push through the crowd
nothing forceful
and nothing persistent.
you don't know where to go from here.
neither do i.

you never understood
why they called it a heavy heart.
it doesn't feel heavy.
it feels more like
an icepick heartache
more like a sprained aorta.
you can feel the limp
every time it beats.
you can feel it
and it doesn't feel heavy
it feels like a pulmonary concussion
like it's been bruised and shaken.
have you ever dropped a snow globe?
it doesn't feel heavy.
it feels like a mitral fracture
like parts that
scientifically
can't even break
but they do anyway
out of sadness
like self-destruction.
your heart doesn't feel heavy
but you wish it did
don't you?
and you wish
they called it something else
something more accurate
because i'm sure you'd take heavy
over any of this.
i'm sure you'd take heavy
over any of this
any day.

09/28/2011

there's this beast
and his hands are broken
and his teeth are sharp
but some are missing
and he'll come to you
thinking you're a hospital
and dammit
you are
you are
so you'll heal him
take him in and make your arms a bed
turn your fingers into iv lines
and nurse him whole
every bone reset
every wound stitched
every missing part replaced
and there he'll stand
beast again
so he'll dig his claws
into your chest
and rip pieces of you
i'm sure you need
and he'll blame you for healing him
and he'll blame you for bleeding
and dammit you'll apologize
you'll apologize
but if you read this in time
then i hope you bite your tongue
and i hope you understand
that your kindness should
never warrant an apology
and anyone who tells your otherwise
is wrong.

|0/20/20||

you always want to be the one
who leaves
but he's threatening that
because for the first time ever
you want to stay
and this vulnerability scares you
so you don't just look for a way out
you make one
with whatever it takes
and by any means necessary
and right now that looks like
an underground tunnel
you've dug with your nails
and he holds your hands and asks
where all the dirt comes from
and why you're always sore
and why you collect plastic spoons
but you just smile and shrug your shoulders.
"i'll tell you tonight" you say
knowing damn well
you'll be gone before
the sun even sets.

10/30/2011

for 12 years
i've been trying to write a poem
that hurts so deeply
one that feels like ice pellets on glass
no
like reaching for the cupboard above the stove
tippy toes and all
but you slip
and your palm lands on open flame
except instead of your palm
i want it to be your everything
i want it all to hurt when you read this
i want emergency room stretchers and sirens
waiting rooms filled at midnight
i want casts and painkillers and blood infusions
i want you to feel something
because god knows i do
every time i try to write this story
but i keep choking
i keep spitting it back up
and thinking
when does
the giver stop giving?
when does
the doctor stop healing?
when does
the lover stop loving
and when does
the hurt stop hurting?

the understanding

you are where you're supposed to be. right? wrong.
but that's okay.

01/06/2012

i wish i could tell you that i'm here
waiting for you
with it all figured out
finally
but i can't.
because i don't.
i'm still scared of the future
and the past still knocks on my door
and the now sometimes feels like a blur
and i'm sorry.
but things are still okay.
people are still good
some of them
but by the time you read this
you'll already know that.
and i'm sorry
but at least i'm writing you this.
it's been sitting on my tongue for a while
i just hope it reaches you when your arms
and mind
are wide open.
i'm sorry i don't have it worked out
but if you stay
maybe we can do it together.

01/15/2012

you worry
you'll never be able to hear
your own thoughts
when there are tvs
and entire orchestras
in your head
drowning out your now.
but those screens
and symphonies
someone told me
they start reciting words
and playing melodies
you'll want to listen to
tap your fingers to
memorize.
someone told me
there will come a day where
the noise
turns into something
you'll actually want to hear.
i just hope they're right.

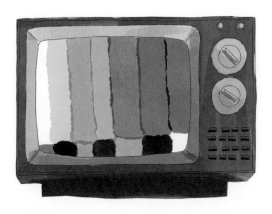

02/23/2012

there's something wrong
with the way you understand love
no
not wrong
different.
and not you
we.
but still.
when they give too much
you don't give at all.
your head gets louder
your mouth gets softer
and your eyes never meet theirs.
but you love anyway
from afar
quietly
and always alone
but it's there.
and then
when they don't love you
or give you anything
when their eyes
stare at everything
but you
you can't look away
can't stop your tongue
from running
because being alone
when no love is given
means
the love you trap inside you
isn't going anywhere
and you haven't understood

how to give it to yourself
yet
which is okay
because you will.
but right now
this one-sided love
is the only thing you know
but that's why i'm here
to tell you that taking love
and giving it
should never be separated
that taking love
and giving it
is the only way this thing
makes sense.
take love
and give it
to her
and him
but first
to yourself.

03/01/2012

remember
please
if there's nothing else you do
just remember.
remember how they hurt you
but don't ever hold it against them.
remember what they said
but forgive them anyway.
remember what you did
but love yourself still.
remember
because
the moment you forget
there will come
a flood of the same mistakes
over and over
and you will welcome them
with open arms.
but i swear
you can't afford
to hurt much more.

05/09/2012

at times like this
you'll try to tell yourself
that the pain can drive you
can take you to places you've never been
but these places aren't always good
and you'll go anyway
and that's where i am right now
in a car
or train
or something
taking me somewhere
i don't really think i want to go
but i'm going because that's what you do
when the pain is this bad
when your heart aches so much
that the hurt
echoes
through every part of you.
you let it take you where it has to
and you pray
to something
to someone
to anything and anyone
that the places it will take you are good
and the people it will drive you to are good
but that isn't always the case
and i haven't figured out yet
what you do when this happens
and how you get home from here
but i will
i know i will
and i'll tell you when i do.

06/14/2012

you won't always make homes out of people.
you'll make them out of kindness
photos
voicemails
and you'll make them out of moments
and you'll make them temporary
because you can't keep visiting places
you can never live
and you can't keep holding on to people
you can never have.

you're losing your memory
so let me help you out with this.
have you figured out what it means
to break
or to be
or what it means to feel
both of these at once?
because i know most of last december is a blur
and the one before that.
god knows what you've missed
but right now you're hurting
and you thought you would recognize this feeling
the breaking
and the being
and the trying to fall apart
without losing the little parts of you
you've held on to.
you've lost your memory though
so none of this is familiar
but you know you've felt it before
you must've.
you have a list too long to tattoo
of everyone who's hurt you
who's made you bleed
made you scream
made you lose your mind.
but this
this is something different.
it's starting to feel like a new list
isn't it?
but this time
you're the one who's doing the hurting
and the list isn't yours.

08/06/2012

you can't write
so by default
you can't breathe either
it's like an entire universe
is building up inside you
but you can't show me it
and i know
it's beautiful
and it's big
and it's growing
but it's hidden
you just don't know
how to uncover it
so you're trying to collect stars
from other universes
you're trying to build flashlights
using nothing but your smile
you're not an engineer
but you're trying to study the circuits
of your heart
because maybe something's disconnected
maybe a wire is missing
and that's why you're here
that's why you're stuck
that's why you can't speak
but nothing seems to be working
and you don't know how much longer
you can last like this.

09/18/2012

i don't know who taught you
that love hurts
that if your heart aches
and your mind is torn
then it's real
because
this is going to make you spend
the next part of your life
searching for pain
to remind you
that you're in love.
and then when you find people
who will finally love you back
you're going to question it
because it won't hurt anymore
and you'll think that must mean
it isn't real
but it is
it has to be
because i don't think
love is supposed to hurt.
i think it's supposed to heal
and i don't know
who taught us
otherwise.

09/27/2012

my poems are all
starting to sound the same.
they blur into each other
the way the traffic lights do
when they reflect on the street
after a rainstorm
and the whole city
lights up at night
and it makes sense
because lately it's
been rainstorm after rainstorm
so why wouldn't these words
get washed into each other?
but i'm worried
that this isn't just happening here
on paper
i'm worried that it's happening
inside me too
because it's getting a little hard
to tell the difference
between feeling too much
and not feeling at all.
so it's kind of like these late-night rainstorms
except the only difference is
there are no coloured lights inside me
to ease the darkness.
but i'm still writing these poems
even though they're all the same
because maybe you need to hear me tell you
it will be okay
in a hundred different ways
until you start believing it.
so here's another poem

that i could've written in 4 words
but instead i chose 203
this time
because maybe you need to hear it
in a hundred different ways
and maybe you need to hear it
in a hundred different words.

10/12/2012

don't read this now.
read this the day you hear your words
in the mouths of people
who were never meant to taste
your thoughts.
don't read this now.
read this the day you realize
you're alone
not physically
you're never really alone
physically
but you are in other ways.
read this when you figure out
what ways i'm talking about.
don't read this now.
read this the day you feel
your teeth
being pulled from your gums
because that's what it will feel like
when you lose the people
you thought you needed.
don't read this now.
it won't make much sense
because you're too trusting
and you're going to be devastated
when you find out
that these people
really want nothing
but to see your downfall
and they will
at any costs
but you'll get up anyway
and when you do

i hope you realize
that sometimes
it's better to just
bite your tongue.
and i hope you don't read this now
because i want you to learn it on your own.

11/01/2012

when you say you feel anxious
i think you mean
there's something inside your chest
clawing its way out
and in the process
it scratches at the organs under your skin
the ones you need to breathe
and be
and this lump in your throat gathers
ties a knot
and sends an anchor to the bottom
of an ocean inside you that
you're too afraid to swim in
and when you say you feel anxious
i hope you teach yourself how to talk to
this thing inside your chest
how to care for it
instead of yell
and how to pat it on the shoulder
and forgive it for being so restless.
i hope you learn how to
love this part of yourself.

02/07/2013

on days you feel like a tornado
you ask god to give you pain.
you ask god to weaken your spirit a little
so you're no longer this force to be reckoned with
so you're no longer destructive and coldhearted.
you then try to muster up the courage
to ask god why he made you a poet.
why you don't breathe like everyone else
why you don't need air to keep you going
why words are all
that have ever kept you alive.
and you imagine he replies with clouds
sending them all to hover around you
and daring you to make them pour
using nothing but your tongue.
you imagine you can.
on days you feel like a tornado
you ask god to help you settle
to hurt you if it means not hurting them
to make you ruin nothing but yourself
because you know you can get back up
but you worry they can't
if you knock them over too hard.
today you feel like a tornado
and you keep telling yourself that
the pain you've been handed
without even asking this time
is a blessing.
it's a blessing.
it's a blessing.
it has to be a blessing.

02/29/2013

the next time you love
don't drown in him.
don't let him be the saltwater ocean
that makes its way into your lungs
until air doesn't taste good anymore.
don't be gentle either.
don't turn your fingers into hooks
for him to hang up his tired
and don't turn your words into band aids.
don't be the pillow he comes home to
when he needs to empty his head
of all his broken.
the next time you love
don't be giving.
be giving
but not in the ways you have been.
don't give him late night stories
or impromptu poems
unless there's an open road
in front of you
and his hand is holding yours
simply out of habit.
don't be giving.
don't sacrifice parts of you
he doesn't want to keep
because that's not how things work.
it's all or nothing.
the next time you love
don't turn him into a metaphor.
don't play connect the dots
with everything he is
and everything
you want him to be.

he should've already drawn those lines
before he met you
and if he didn't
then just don't fall in love.
the next time you love
don't let him get away with much
because this isn't a game of cops and robbers
that you're trying to drag out until sunset
so you don't have to go home.
you can go home if you want to
whether or not this game ends early.
the loneliness doesn't scare you anymore.
so he either wins or he doesn't.
there's no bending the rules
this time around.
the next time you love
don't
unless you're sure it's really love.

03/05/2013

if love is everything he taught you it was
then i hope you never feel it again.
if love is sacrificing parts of yourself
you never thought you'd live without
or yelling words
you never thought you'd pronounce
at 4:00 in the morning on a weekday
then love just isn't for us.
i don't want to be in love.
i don't want you to be either.
instead
i hope we stay stuck in a state
of worry-less confusion
where all the things we feel
when he's around
get cluttered together
and sadness no longer looks like sadness
and happiness rubs off
on every anxious part of us
like cheap jeans on new leather.
i hope i never fall in love
and i hope you don't either
at least not now.
at least not until
we understand
what love is.

03/31/2013

in this story
you're not a jasmine flower
and he doesn't pretend to know
how to hold you without ripping your petals.
he doesn't dial your number
at 6:00 am
and even if he did
you wouldn't pick up
because you know better.
except this story isn't real
and you do pick up
you always pick up
and he has pretty words
and you are easy to fool
and naive
and you fall
and you keep falling
and you never stick the landing
and it hurts
my god it hurts
but if this story was real
if we pretended
for just a minute
that this story was real
he'd be a trampoline
and you'd be sky high
and the fall wouldn't break you apart
like it always does.

you touch him
like a highway exists between you
like he's on the other side
maybe in a small blue volkswagen
and you're on foot
walking against traffic
no
scratch that
on rollerblades
skating your way toward him
but for once
this busy city isn't so busy
the roads are clear
and he doesn't check his mirrors.
you touch him
like he's a green light
away from disappearing
like he is the green light
the one that shines across the pier.

05/05/2013

you'll try to write a poem about him
but the only ones you know how to write
are either unrealistically optimistic
or terribly heartbreaking.
but he isn't any of those things.
he isn't a love poem either though.
he's not an evening of journaling
or an early morning banter
between your hands and your tongue.
he's not the strength of your voice
when you perform pieces
you don't even remember writing
and he isn't the silence of your pages
when you try to run away from all the noise.
but he isn't the noise either.
you're going to try to write a poem about him
but he's everything unfamiliar
and you are only just learning
how to stop your knees from buckling
and your hands from shaking
every time you hold something
as breathtakingly unordinary
because you're a klutz
and you always seem to fumble the things
you only ever wanted to hold on to.
so you'll try to learn
how to stop your everything from panicking
every time you hold something
you don't want to fumble.
i know you're a klutz but please
just this time
don't fumble.

05/16/2013

i hope he understands
that sometimes your tongue
turns into a thousand pieces of glass
and you bleed every time you try to speak.
on days like this
you will still try to tell him every story
you can think of
because you like the taste of pain
reminding you that you can break
and you can heal
and you can be
all at once.
there are days where your hands
turn into the twisted cords on old telephones
knotted and tangled in the parts of you
you've been meaning to get rid of
the parts of you
you've been meaning to pack tightly
in boxes labelled *donate*
but you haven't
and they're still sprawled
on the bedroom floor
mountains of a you
you don't want anymore
mountains of a you
someone else might need
and i hope he understands
it will take time to find the tape
to close up the boxes
to untangle your limbs
to bandage your tongue.
it will take time
and i hope he understands.

every time you say "forever"
you want to pour bleach
down your throat
because he's not forever
and you're not broken anymore.

08/17/2013

i know you want to be
unmoved by this
unwavering
you want to be the kid
who sticks her tongue to the metal pole
the one who doesn't wear the snow pants
the careless one
i know you want to
place it all between your jaws
let your incisors bite down
spit it out
blood teeth and all
and still
you want to be indifferent.
you want it all to not matter.
you want them to not matter.
but it does
and they do
but you do too.
you matter too.

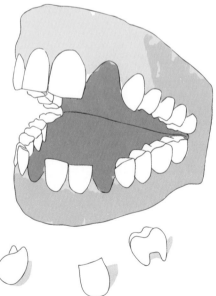

your wear happiness
like you wear hand-me-downs:
clearly not yours
and clearly uncomfortable.
you wear it
like you're shopping for something better
like you're just holding on to it
until you don't have to anymore
and you do this because it's unfamiliar
because it's nothing you're used to
because it never fits right
never hugs your shoulders the way it should
or grips your waist the way it should.
the happiness is always one size too big
one size too small
not the right colour
ripped at the seams
and you never learned to sew
or how to tailor these things
into something better
how to dip it all in tie dye
wring it out
and wait for it to dry.
you never learned how to turn happiness
into something that looks good on you.
but you will.
give it some time
and you will.

11/04/2013

you heard her voice once
and remembered a different time.
you remembered water gun fights
and bright red popsicles
lemonade stands that never made a dollar
but somehow always ran out of stock
and night lights
you remembered night lights
and the huge curtain-less window
that was pushed up against your bed
moonlight always sneaking in
to listen to your late-night conversations
laughs concealed in pillows
doors opening too loudly
and then the morning coffee
the morning coffee
that always made you wonder
what it'd feel like
to scrape off taste buds
rearrange them like lego pieces
make them feel like something new.
you heard her name once
and you remembered what it felt like
to be holy
to be pure
to be untouched by sadness
untouched by misery.
you heard her name once
and your wounds started to chant
like a church choir on sunday morning
and they only sang of her.
you heard her name once
and learned

for the first time ever
what it meant to love
what it meant to be so intertwined
in something other than your heartache.
but now
now you hear her name
and shut your eyes
press your palms to your ears
and drown her out.
there's no one left to remember.
there's nothing left to love.

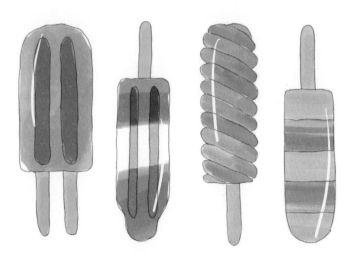

12/26/2013

you hold love in your mouth
like it's contraband
like you've been wrongfully imprisoned
and are forced to carry
razor blades beneath your tongue.
you skip over the word
like mud after a rainstorm
like white shoes and deep puddles
like storm clouds
when the weatherman said otherwise.
you skip over the word like
"where's my raincoat?
have you seen my umbrella?"
like scrambling before work
because you didn't realize
it was going to pour
until you got out there
had to run 2 blocks back
elevator's broken
40 something flights of stairs.
you arrive out of breath
but it doesn't matter anyway
because you're always out of breath
when it comes to him
so your lungs are used to the feeling already
but your heart isn't.
it isn't used to the pounding
the different kind
the one that worsens
every time he smiles
and you're scared
so the first thing you do
is run your tongue

over the weaponry you keep hidden
to remind yourself that you're safe
to reassure your organs
that there's an army in place
that you can fight back if need be
and i'm sure you can
but who taught you that you need to?
who taught you that love is war?
and why do you still believe them?

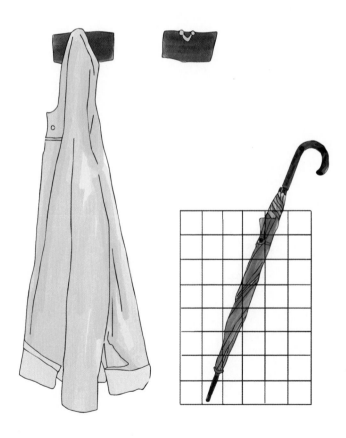

12/28/2013

not every poem i write is about her.
this one isn't
it's about you
and how there's something wrong
with the way your heart's been beating
because lately
it's been beating in morse code
spells out her name
first and last
and the doctors
haven't figured out why yet.
so i guess this poem is about her
after all
but it's also about you
and how you're
trying to change this rhythm
trying to break free of her song
trying to break free of her hold
trying to forget how gullible you were
telling yourself that you aren't to blame
that you were never the reason
she hurt herself
that she only wanted
to point a finger at you
because she was too afraid
to point it at herself
so now you're trying to heal
by turning into something
that doesn't need someone
into someone that doesn't need her.
and for the first time in a long time
i think it's working.
i think it doesn't faze you anymore.

the lies she told
the blame she gave
the feeling too much
the feeling more than her
the giving
the giving
the giving
and of course
the hurting
goddamn it
the hurting.
but i think it doesn't faze you anymore.

the growing

i'm here now. not there. not where i was before.
i'm here. still falling. still hurting. still bleeding
words. but you're here too. so stay for a while
longer. stay so you can watch me save myself.
stay because things are about to get a whole
lot better. stay because i'm about to get
a whole lot better.

every poem i've written is missing words
missing meaning.
there's something i'm trying to say
but none of it sounds poetic
none of it sits well on the tongue
so i've tried to twist it all
tried to stir the dictionary the way
i stir the morning tea i can never finish.
i'm writing poems i can never finish
i'm feelings things that won't ever end
so screw the poem
screw the trying to make it sound nice
screw making the bed
fluffing the pillows
folding the blankets
if it doesn't sit well
then let it stand
screw the hospitality
these are the missing words:
i have been trying to tell you
that i don't want to feel what i feel
that i overthink
that i overdo
and that i don't regret any of it.
that i eat skittles because
parts of me are so bitter
i'm convinced the sugar
will somehow melt into me
that my body will absorb
only the sweet parts
and you won't have to
taste the harshness
i've hidden so well.

so screw the poem
i just want to tell you
that i don't want to feel what i feel
but even that isn't coming out right
because those words aren't strong enough
they don't tell you how i grind my bones at night
create this dust out of all my broken
swallow it
and hope to regrow new limbs
that haven't been to the places i've been
but it never works.
instead i'm bent over on my knees
throwing up every attempt to recreate myself
so screw the poem.
screw the poem that never says
what i want it to say.

03/19/2016

the summer of 2008
looked a little more like an ice storm.
you heard words
that should've only belonged
in graveyards
funeral homes
hospital beds.
you heard them more times
than you heard
your mother's maiden name.
you craved their sound
but your voice still cracked
every time your tongue
prepared itself for them.
the summer of 2008
was a little less than perfect.
i lied.
a lot less.
but the endless phone calls
and the sirens
screamed
the words you needed to hear
not the graveyard ones
but the growing garden
empty forests
flowing waterfall ones.
the hopeful ones.
they told you
"it'll pass. it'll pass"
and when you screamed back
you said "i know"
even though
you didn't have a damn clue.

04/14/2016

you're going to lose her
and him
and yourself
"but it will be so beautiful"
they say.
like scattering the pieces of who you are
around the universe
hoping someone will find them
create a map of you
and fall in love.
hoping someone will listen to your story
the way you listen for the ocean
in shells you rummage through the sand for.
hoping someone will put you back together
mail you everything you lost along the way
so you can be whole again.
but your trips to the post office
are only leaving you emptier than before.
you're relying on someone out there
to recreate you
to build you up again
to make you better than you were.
but you can do it all yourself.

you're going to cry away december
in the empty forest
you never walked through
because you knew better.
and when you get there
you're going to enter
axe in hand
ready to tear down the trees
you watched grow
every time you took the long way
because you didn't want to disturb the monsters
you thought lived inside that place
but they didn't
they lived inside you
and you know that now.
but you do this out of rage
because you've lost everything
you've ever held dear
and this is how you let it all out
so you're going to tear apart the beehives
and listen to them scream
for their home that no longer exists.
"you are like me"
you'll tell them
"i do not have a home either
but at least you can fly."
and then suddenly
you'll fall.
you'll dig your nails into the dirt
lean against the boulders
and hear a familiar voice somewhere
telling you that
what lies inside this forest is

too heavy for you
too big for you
too painful for you to carry.
and when you hear this
i need you to scream back
i need you to speak into the emptiness
that surrounds you
and say
"i'll find love here
because it hides in the things that are
too heavy for me
too big for me
too painful for me to carry
and when i do
i'll wrap my arms around it
ask it if it's lost
and tell love that it can stay with me
if it is
and we can build a new home together."

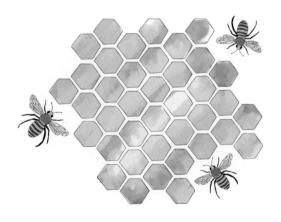

06/10/2016

walking away from her
was the first step you took
toward healing
since the day her tornado
met your earthquake
and caused disaster.
don't ever be sorry for it.

may your sadness
be your north star
may it help you
find your way back
to tomorrow
may it act as your parachute
not your anchor.
feel it
but don't let it take you over.
learn to love it
accept it
but don't let it build a home
inside you.
let it be
like your first love
there
but only for a little while.
and like your first love
let it go.
you are better off.

05/22/2017

when you wake up one morning
half the bed untouched
while your half
the aftermath of a restlessness
you never thought you'd feel
get up anyway.
learn to live without.
because things
or people
or feelings
stay
or they go.
they're either here
or they're not.
and most times
the not wins.
but you learn
how to live anyway
how to let go
without losing yourself
how to adapt to loneliness
and to a new kind of quiet.
you start making tea instead of coffee
pouring in half a bottle of honey
and downing your boiling mug
like it's the lemonade
your mother used to make for you.
you paint your room white
instead of the blue it was.
you hang up new posters
take new pictures
to replace the ones
you can no longer look at.

this is what you do when they leave.
things
or people
or feelings.
you get up
and you learn to live without.

after caitlyn siehl's "it ends or it doesn't"

to be at peace while running.
to like running.
to rip pieces out
and not bleed
to not want to bleed.
to bite your tongue
and pull out teeth.
to not need them anyway.
to not want them back.
to be the tin man.
to erase your past
without erasing you.
to be okay.
to stop believing in this
mudslide of maybes
and to still be okay.

at first
love was something
you thought you knew inside out
like the way your hands
know their way around empty canvases.
you thought you knew
that love was empathetic
that it was fullness
that it was gentle.
but the years challenged you
they tried to convince you
that love couldn't stitch your wounds
that love couldn't cure your tiredness
that love couldn't bring you happiness.
and you thought the years
just might've been right.
but believe me
there is love here
somewhere
the good kind
the kind that won't stitch your wounds
but instead makes you numb to the hurt
the kind that won't cure your tiredness
but instead makes you never want to sleep
the kind that won't bring you happiness
but instead gives you the courage
to create it on your own.
look for this love.
and hold it when you find it.

i want to tell you more than anything
that good people stay
but they don't
and i'm still trying to figure out
if that means they aren't good
or if you aren't good
no
scratch that
you are good
you are more than good.
you are enough.
but i'm still trying to figure out
why they leave
where they go
and when they'll come back
no
scratch that
if they'll come back.
i want to tell you more than anything
that good people stay
but they don't.
i can tell you though
that you don't need them.
that you only need you.
that you are whole
and full
all on your own.
that you aren't someone's better half
or someone's missing puzzle piece.
you are whole
and full
you are two sides of a coin

black and white
wood and fire
perfect
and imperfect.
i want to tell you more than anything
that good people stay
but they don't.
and you don't need them anyway.

09/07/2017

there are times
i want to sit down
and write you an entire encyclopedia
maybe map out the next 10 years for you
tell you which shortcuts not to take
and which turns to avoid
because finding your way in the dark
is anything but easy.
but i never do.
i'm sorry that you're travelling blindly
and i'm sorry that i'm there
staring.
"careful"
i whisper
"watch your step."
but i know you can't hear me.
i never wrote you an encyclopedia
or drew you a map
but i'm writing you this
to tell you that you'll make it
that it never really is the end of the road
no matter how dark it may seem.

they'll shame sadness
like it's a misspelled tattoo
and then wonder why your smile
is never as real as it should be.
or as it used to be.
but either way
they'll tell you to hide your broken parts
to rub makeup over your scars
plant flowers on your tongue
to stop your words
from sounding like swords.
"you aren't perfect"
they'll say.
"but you will be
once your laugh is a little louder
a little more believable."
but they're wrong.
"you aren't perfect"
they'll say
over and over
until it starts to sound
like that radio tune you hate
but can't get out of your head.
and when they do
i need you to scream
"i am i am i am.
sadness and all.
i am perfect."

you'll heal suddenly and overnight.
you'll heal when you fall in love
with new colours and new cities.
when you stop listening to sad songs
and start listening to your thoughts
instead of running away from them.
you'll heal when you stop running.
when you stop running from the noise
and from the past
and from the happiness.
you'll start healing the day you stop
loving the people you shouldn't love.
and the day you start loving yourself.

when you were a girl
you wanted to dig
for the things
you couldn't find in others
or yourself
or anywhere.
but now you have more
than your hands
can carry.
and you'll wonder
what strengthens bone
what heals broken skin?
and you'll ask
"why can't my veins
withstand all the weight?"
you'll turn to eveyone
who's hurt you
and say
"have you seen my blame
my guilt
my damage?
have you seen all the things
i found digging through dirt?
and would you call it treasure?"
no matter what they say
the answer is yes.
yes. yes. yes.
i would call it gold.

after misha abarbanel's "archeology"

12/09/2017

he's a mixture of too loud
and mostly quiet all at once
and you'll figure this out
when you talk and talk
because silence never sits
quite well with you does it
and he doesn't say much back
but you can see his eyes
and they're studying you
with so much noise
and you can see his smile
and it reminds you
of the streets back home
on graduation day
and this screws with you a little
because he's standing right in front of you
and you're okay
with hearing your voice only for once
and it's because you feel safe here.
but you look around
and nothing is familiar
it isn't home
but it sure as hell feels like it
and this is the part of the story
where i apologize
over and over
because this is where
you lose yourself
for the first time ever
and this time
i can't spoil the ending for you.

02/11/2018

when the sadness arrives
invite it in
before it has a chance
to ring the doorbell.
tell it you've been
waiting for it to come.
check your watch once
and then don't check it again.
make small talk.
then talk big.
and while you do this
the happiness will eavesdrop
and the happiness will get antsy.
let it.
but do not ask it to leave.

03/09/2018

i'm sorry that everything
you've read thus far
has been heart-wrenching.
i don't think i'm being fair.
life hasn't been all that bad
even though i've painted it to be
it really hasn't.
there have been times
we drove up to the middle of nowhere
with nothing but a telescope
and all the world's happiness
and the windows were down
even though you couldn't feel your fingers
but we saw the stars that night
and our hearts swelled up
and our eyes grew bigger
and everything was calm.
and there have been times
good ones
like when we walked down that road
for seven hours
reading poetry
with our cellphones off
because for the next few years
there won't be much quiet anywhere
in your head
or your heart
or your palms
but it's okay
because there will be times like these
that will help you remember
why you're even here
reading this

and you're going to smile
and let your chest fall
and your eyes draw shut
and for the first time
in a long time
you'll realize that everything
really will be okay.

i know what it's like to drown
in everything but water
in guilt and blame and worry
and it's because i'm too gullible
and you are too
and i know what it's like to drown
because i never took the time
to learn to swim
because i never really knew
i was even drowning
until my lungs filled with everything but air
and i couldn't breathe
and more importantly
i couldn't speak
and it's your turn now
you're drowning as you read this
you're gasping for air but there is none
or maybe there is
but it has a mind of its own
and it's making you fight for it
because nothing comes easy
and you'll learn this one when
you're on your bedroom floor
wondering why
living is so hard
and it can be
sometimes
you're right
but it's only because
it's worth it
and nothing that's worth it
ever comes easy.

04/17/2018

i know it's sadistic
but i'm kind of excited
for the day you realize
they never loved you
or loved you
only because it was
good for them
not you
it was never because of you
and i know it's sadistic
but just hear me out.
we only learn when it's too late
through shattered screens
car accidents
heartbreaks.
we only learn when it's too late
so nothing i say
will stop you from getting this part of you
broken
because it's inevitable
but you'll learn
my god will you learn.

you're going to go through people
like they're the outfits you try on
the morning of the party
you actually want to go to for once.
and this is okay.
but when you're left with a pile
of worn out things
tired mountains
growing on your bedroom floor
know that a few years from now
you're going to meet someone
who will drive you out
to the middle of nowhere
park the car
on the side of the road
and let you scream your lungs out
to release some of the pain
and she'll laugh
and she'll cry
and she'll tell you
she can't hear you
even though
her ears will be ringing
and her head will be loud
because she doesn't really
like noise
but she'll do it
because she loves you
selflessly
sometimes too selflessly
but she loves you
and that's what matters.

05/15/2018

so here we are
where we were bound to end up
broken heart
but somehow still as whole as ever.
this is where you always get stuck.
this is where you always lose the words
when you don't know what to tell her
to make her realize
that she's the most beautiful damn thing
you've ever seen.
no
scratch that
the most beautiful damn thing
this world's ever seen.
so here we are.
this is what you need to tell her.
"i hope you pick out the shrapnel
he left in your skin
because he was a ticking time bomb
from the beginning
but this is okay.
we get up anyway and we learn.
i hope you use the broken pieces
to build something new.
i hope you use melted gold
instead of glue
and i hope you remember
that broken doesn't last forever
and that they make mosaics out of things like you
because you're the most beautiful damn thing
this world's ever seen."

05/25/2018

i don't want to guide you.
i don't want to be the person
standing on the side of the street
of your childhood home
handing you a map of the town you grew up in
thinking you don't know your way around.
you know your way around.
so i'll let you roam
wander
get lost
even when the paths you take are covered
in tears and blood
that belong to me.
and you'll recognize it too.
you'll smell my scent as you walk through
but you won't turn around
because you know
these are mistakes you need to make
or maybe they aren't even mistakes.
but i can't figure that out for you.
instead
i'll walk down nightmare lane for you.
i'll revisit all the pain i've felt
just to show you
that you can make it out alive.
because i made it out alive
didn't i?
and you will too.
i won't tell you
that you're going the wrong way either
because you might not be.
you might be headed exactly
where you're supposed to go.

i can't be your guide.
pain is good
broken is good
it will remind you that you can heal
and you'll get good poetry out of it too.
but i'll be there for you
in case you bleed
in case the hurt
is too much for you to handle.
i'll be there for you
with chocolate
and tickets to anywhere
but i promise
i'll still let you lead the way.

for mel

this is about the fall of 2014.
this is about how you were
a glass-bottom boat on white water currents.
how the splash zone
reached further than arm's length
or heart's length actually
and how the recovery period
was spent in bed for weeks
except no doctors could find the hurt
or diagnose the pain.
they couldn't see it
but you could feel it
you could feel it
and it hurt like a broken rib
on a roller coaster ride
with more upside down loops
than you could count on your fingers.
and then it hurt like
"i don't love you"
except you were the one saying it
over and over
"i don't love you
i don't love you"
and it broke you.
and then it hurt like
swallowing nails
thinking if they couldn't fix you
then maybe you could fix yourself
but you couldn't
not like that.
and now
at least now you know better
at least now you've learned.

the fall of 2014 felt like
ripping out organs
gift wrapping them
ribbon and all
and handing them to people
who didn't want to get their hands dirty.
but hurting means healing
and if glass shard wounds
and bloody clothes
are what you needed to figure that out
then today
today i'm thankful for the fall of 2014.

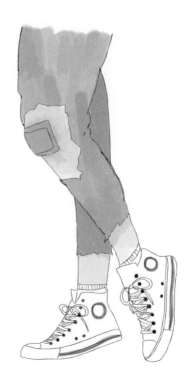

you have arms that want to hoard
and throw away
all at once.
you have arms like tangled wires
like safety lock seatbelts
like shirts that shrink in the wash
on picture day
like bad timing
like broken necklaces
and closed jewelers.
you have arms like
things that don't last
as long as they should
but you have a heart like evening tea
the one with coconut milk and honey
like weekends
like birthdays
like airplane tickets.
you have have arms like magnets
for anything broken
but my god your heart is warm.

after caitlyn siehl's "mouth"

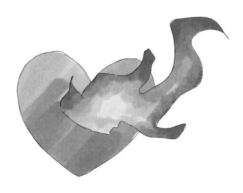

07/20/2018

pop quiz.
what do you call someone
who gives but doesn't take?
do you call them kind
or do you call them selfless?
trick question.
neither.
you call them scared
and sometimes
you call them broken.
i used to be exactly that.
i used to open my hands
palms faced upwards
eyes locked
on the way my fingers trembled
as they took and took and took.
i was not kind and i was not selfless.
but things have changed
and i take now.
i take love when it's given
and i take help when it's needed
i take time when it's called for
and i take band aids when i'm bleeding.
so
makeup quiz.
what do you call someone
who gives and gives and gives
but sometimes takes?
growing.
i would call her growing.

08/16/2018

i once heard about an art
where shattered glass
is mended back together
with melted gold.
but i don't want to
mend you back together
with melted gold.
you are the gold.
and you don't need mending.
instead
i want to hug you in ways
that make you forget
that the human body
contains 206 bones
that can all be broken
in different ways
and different places.

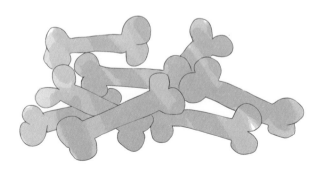

08/29/2018

when you find him
tell him to
read you your future
like he's reading you his favourite book
or showing you his favourite song.
tell him to recite it
like he does those textbooks
he's been studying
for as long as he can remember.
tell him you want to hear
the longing in his voice
almost as if he's flipping through
a photo album of his life
that he's never seen before
a nostalgic feeling of something
he once knew
maybe in another lifetime
but definitely not here
because here
doesn't have miracles like this.
tell him to paint you a portrait
but to only use your favourite colours
tell him you want to see if he can recreate
the marks he's left on your heart
and tell him you want to see
if he can breathe light
into every description of you
just by saying your name
in a way that makes him forget
he has lungs.

i want to hear about
a day in the life of us
the same way you'd tell me about
a dream you had
but woke up
too early from
only the waking up
is the dream
and the day in the life of us
becomes us trying
to live our entire lives in a day
and i've done it before
i swear
in every word i've said to you
in every word you've said to me
i've lived an entire life with you
and you're the universe
and every beautiful thing in it.

one day
you'll find the one
who stays up late at night
until the world is silent
just to hear the grasshoppers
ringing through the neighborhood
wondering
how the hell
you hate the sound.
you'll find the one
who won't just ask you how your day was
but how your childhood was
how your future will be
and why you're unhappy with your now
and what you're going to do about it.
you'll find the one
who won't memorize the words
to your favourite songs
but who will read through your poems
like they're holy.
wait for this.

09/17/2018

i wonder what you look like on a bad day.
i wonder if getting out of bed
sounds more like falling
sounds more like sirens on the side of a highway
sounds more like someone sending help.
i wonder what you look like fragile
how easily you break apart
or if you break apart at all.
i mean you must.
there are bad days in us all
so you must
but i wonder if you shatter
like overbaked cookies do
leaving pieces that won't ever fit together again
or if you're something more like ancient dry wall
does your plaster come undone?
and if it does
so what?
have you never been missing before?
i have
and it isn't so bad
if you're missing
if there are voids inside you
if there are parts of you
that are empty
then you have room
for better things
like flakes of gold
and people who call you at 6:00 am
to tell you it's a snow day
and love.
you have more room for love.

the day you meet him
you'll want to travel to every city he's been in
walk with your head glued to the ground
searching for his footprints in the concrete
and retracing his every step
so you can understand where he's been
and maybe collect hints along the way
to try and figure out where he's going.
but you can't.
so instead
i think you'll tattoo the world map on your back
shade in every country you visit
with colours that don't exist
so he can run his fingers across your skin
and see everything you've seen
and feel everything you've felt.
but you can't.
so instead
you'll talk to him until the sun comes up
even if he falls asleep
and you'll tell him stories
and listen to his
and maybe that'll be enough
and you won't need worldwide scavenger hunts
or tattoos that run into your veins
because it'll be enough.
it'll be enough.
i hope you find this
and i hope it's enough.

if you want to know if he's the right one
ask him first if you make his heart race.
does he get nervous?
does he like to see you smile?
i mean
does his brain jump when you do?
does he think before he speaks to you?
part of me hopes he does
and the other part hopes he doesn't.
ask him though
if he likes spending time with you.
i mean
doing nothing
but also doing everything.
and if the answer is yes
does he like it the same way he likes
strawberry ice cream
and expensive leather jackets?
does he ever look at you
and watch time skip ahead?
if he does
what does it look like?
are you laughing
or are you arguing
or both?
and does he ever hit rewind
and rewatch old memories?
i hope he does
because i know you do
you do
and even if he doesn't
i know you hit rewind enough times already
for the both of you.

but does he thank god
or the universe
or his feet
for taking all the rights steps
that have led him to you?
and if so
does he do this enough?
do you do this enough?
have you found the right way yet?
have you found the right words?
write him a poem
or draw him a picture
or talk to him until the seasons change
anything that says
"thank you
thank you
thank you
for all the things you've done for me
and for all the things i know you'll still do."

10/03/2018

i keep wondering
why we give away parts of ourselves
that we actually need.
i used to have this bad habit
that i simply called
"loving the right way"
where i told people that
i loved them with all my heart.
but i don't love them
with all my heart anymore.
i don't ever want to either
and i wouldn't call that
"loving the right way."
i'd call it reckless
and dependent
and something more like
playing hide and seek
in an open field.
i don't love this way now.
i love in different ways
in ways that are kinder
in ways that help me nurse myself
and in ways that keep me whole.
and if love ever had a right or wrong
if there was ever any part of love
that followed rules
or routines
or some sort of universal code
then this would be it.
this would be how to love the right way.

here
in my hands
is this treasure chest collection
of the things i want to give you.
old poetry on napkins
band aids
words that have fallen from my mouth
but not far enough for any ear to hear.
here
lies everything i'm afraid of.
everything i want you to see
but don't want you to see.
everything i want to tell you
but don't want you to know.
everything i want you to tell me
but wonder if you ever will.
here
right here
lies the time i've wasted
on people who didn't deserve it
and here
i wonder if you'll do the same
waste your time on me
or with me.
here
i wonder
if you have a
treasure chest collection too
and if you do
will i ever get to see it?

12/27/2018

i've been wondering
how to describe love to you
because i told you before
that i wasn't really sure
but i kind of have an idea now.
i saw someone today
just an ordinary man
drinking an ordinary coffee
but he made this face
after taking the first sip
and even though it was 8:00 am
on a gloomy tuesday morning
it still made me giggle
and the first thing i wanted to do
was tell him about it.
i think that's love.

01/21/2019

there's something about his hands.
how they remind you of those plants
that twirl the way snakes do
wrapping themselves around anything.
there's something about his smile too
kind of like peach applesauce
hitting the back of your throat
after a long day of yelling at people
you only want to hug
because you see your soft rebellion in them.
you see it in him too.
mostly when he tells you
you aren't doing good enough.
and he doesn't say it
because you aren't doing good enough.
he says it because good enough isn't good enough.
there's something about his past
something comforting
how he's only been to places you haven't
and don't really intend on going.
but there's something comforting about that.
how you know you aren't missing out
because he already has stories
and souvenirs
and red pins to mark it all.
you do too though
but from different places
he probably won't go either
because there's just something about him.
something different.
something new
something like roads less travelled.
there's just something.

01/25/2019

you're going to dream of him
and wake up
with a deck of cards up your sleeve
to try to prove
you're made of magic.
out of habit
you'll cough up poems
spit them out into the sink
and try to shake off words
that taste of bitter coffee
and him.
but you like bitter coffee.
you also like museums
and gardens
and illusions
and you'll learn
just by the way he says your name
that he does too.
you're going to dream of him
and wake up feeling around the room
in the dark
for your inhaler
because when he smiles
your lungs mistake the air for smoke.
he'll tell you to breathe
but your tongue will panic
blurt out an incoherent sentence
but it will make him laugh
and he'll stand a little closer.
you're going to dream of him
and in this dream
i swear he'll look into your eyes
and see a phoenix.

i swear he'll smell the fire
and watch you brush off ashes
and in this dream
i swear he won't hold you
like you're broken.
i swear he won't play 52 pickup
when you hug him and he realizes
the memories you're trying to hold on to
are now scattered on the floor
and in this dream
you're made of magic
and don't need to prove it.

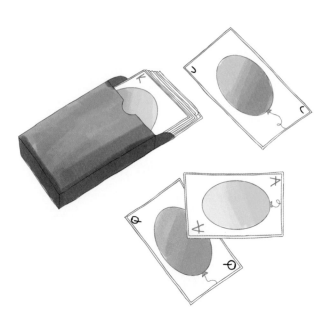

02/02/2019

the longer you stare at him
the more he starts to look like a cliché
like a bad love poem
you'd probably find written on a dirty napkin
in some old coffee shop
you only visit on days you crave noise.
those days are few and far between.
so you shift your attention to something else
grab his hand tighter
and sift through his fingers
like they're a deck of cards
and you're a magician with a few tricks up your
sleeve.
but you're not.
and the only tricks you have
are disappearing and breaking people in two.
does that count?
the longer you stare at him
the more he starts to look like a cliché
but he is nothing of the sort.
so you begin thinking in metaphors
and his eyes turn into the windows on an airplane
the entire sky shining through
and everyone's shoving elbows for a glance.
his heartbeat quickens
causing turbulence and forcing your arms
to turn into seatbelts
and suddenly
you're carrying a ticket to somewhere
and a passport with your name on it
and the entire universe
reconfigures itself into a bucket list
each country a small box

waiting to be checked off.
he is getting out of hand.
he becomes a metaphor
or a simile
or an analogy
and you start
frantically ripping dictionary pages
in search of words worthy enough
but none are
and you're left with nothing
but the spine of a book
limbs torn completely
and you wonder if this is it.
the not-so-cliché way he makes you feel
limbless
a poet with no words on her tongue
a magician with no tricks up her sleeve
a book with no pages.
he becomes a metaphor
and for the first time ever
your words aren't
big enough
loud enough
don't hold enough meaning
to describe everything he is
and this should scare you
but for the first time ever
it won't.

he wants you to love him
like your lungs love air
but that isn't good enough
is it?
you want something stronger
something more like
"i love you the way i love weekends:
desperately and with everything i have."
no actually
"i love you like yellow rain boots
and coats that keep me dry
when i face the storm."
scratch that
try this:
"i love you like good music
on long country car rides"
like "can you roll the window down?"
and "pull over so i can
dance on the side of the street."
something more like
"let's leave our car parked here
walk nowhere and
see if it all still
feels the same at sunrise"
and "i love you
like tire tracks on dirt roads
like longing
like fulfillment."
or try this:
"i don't love you like
lungs love air because
i don't love you like necessity.
i love you like privilege."

02/12/2019

he's the kind of light you'll only read about
in sci-fi novels.
you know
the one where 40 red suns shine against the earth
except the earth is a sphere made of mirrors
so the light shines back
bounces off anything and everything
and before you know it
the universe turns into a kaleidoscope.
i've never been good at science though
so i'm not sure if that's exactly how it works
but do you understand?
do you understand that
he's a light that doesn't play by the rules
one that leaks into the darkness
one that will leak into your darkness.
do you understand?
do you understand that
you'll start collecting jars
the day you meet him
that you'll start letting fireflies free
trying to chase him like you chased them
trying to keep him with you
so you can stare at his light up close
in awe
and thankful.
in awe and forever thankful.
do you understand?

02/14/2019

in your dream
you fall asleep on the kitchen floor
using the heat of the oven to keep you warm.
you leave the blinds up
and let the leftover rush hour traffic
sink into the windows
but in your dream
the windows are made of sugar
and you're on the highest floor
and you're not afraid of heights
and in your dream
you wake up to the smell
of french toast and chocolate chips.
he grabs the maple syrup
while you let the dishes stay dirty
let the bed stay unmade
let the past stay messy
let the future stay hidden.
he grabs the maple syrup
while you
for the first time
just let it all be
and in your dream
you eat through your sugar windows
and you keep the oven on
and pretend it's your own little fireplace
even though it's spring outside
and you let the days bleed into each other
and you throw out calendars
and you throw out clocks
and you just let it all be.
and in your dream
there are no scientific rules

and there are no dictionaries either
so in this dream
if you were to tell him you love him
you'd say something like
"have you ever heard of a lion?
have you ever seen an elephant?
imagine a lion as big as an elephant
as heavy
and imagine it roar
in an empty place.
can you hear the echo?
can you hear the noise?"
and in this dream
he'd know exactly what you're talking about
and he'd smile and say
"i elephant-sized lion roar you too."

03/13/2019

this is a poem about a feeling
i can't put my finger on.
this is a poem about someone
i don't remember anymore
about a number
i don't recognize anymore
about a name
i can't pronounce anymore.
this is a poem about
what comes after the healing.
this is the best part of the story.
this is the part i've been waiting for
the one that tastes like morning coffee
and afternoon ice cream
while watching the snow blow
from the top floor of an apartment
you snuck into
because it's the highest one in town
and this is a poem about
the way you can breathe now
despite it all
the way you can breathe
without feeling like
an entire year's worth
of overfilled journals
are collapsing your lungs
and this is the poem
that comes after the healing
the one about blueberries
and flowers
and love
about how they grow in parts of you
you were convinced had already died.

these are the letters i write
to the person i was.
these are words that sometimes taste
like blood in mouth
like sucker punch
like losing
but they also taste like candied apples
and watching the sun rise from an airplane window
and hope.
these are the letters i write
to the person i was
and this
this is the poem i write
to the person i'll be
and when it reaches her
i know she'll turn into a sunflower
if she hasn't already
and i know she'll wipe the blood
that drips from her lips
and spit out all the sadness
and i know she'll draw a map
pinpoint every city she's escaped to
and unlace her shoes
because i know she won't need them anymore
because she doesn't need to escape anymore
and i know when this poem reaches her
she won't know how to speak
anything but a "thank you"
to all the pain
and all the hurt
and all the years of being broken.
she won't know how to speak
anything but a "thank you."